This book belongs to

Share your colored versions with us! We love seeing your results and hearing from you we are social!

The Official FB book page, stay on top of what we have in the works!
www.facebook.com/globaldoodlegems
The Community group, share your colored pages, meet the artists, enjoy exclusive freebies, take part in community Charity books and so much more......
www.facebook.com/groups/globaldoodlegems/
Follow us on Twitter.... @GlobalDoodlegem
We are on Instagram too
@globaldoodlegems for instagram
...and if you are not social like that we have a blog
globaldoodlegems.wordpress.com

Copyright © 2017 Global Doodle Gems
All rights are reserved by Global Doodle Gems.
Duplication of pages for personal use are allowed. You are invited to color the pages then scan/post your coloured versions to social networks, mentioning the book title and author/artist (Global Doodle Gems).
All artwork and images are protected by copyright laws. This book or any portion thereof may not, otherwise, be reproduced and/or distributed or transmitted without the express written permission of the artist/publisher of Global Doodle Gems.
All of us from the Global Doodle Gems wish you a colortastic time and look forward to seeing your wonderful color results online!

I am an average career woman juggling the demands of family and work. After an illness, I had difficulty controlling my hand and could not even hold a pen. I used drawing as physical therapy and rehabilitation for my hand. When I experience discomfort, drawing and coloring relax me, both physically and mentally, bringing me into the world of art. At the same time, I discovered that art has awakened the child in me. This inner child reflects my state of mind. Thanks to the art friends in Taiwan, our mutual encouragement of each other, and Maria's assistance, I finally have an opportunity to share the fruits of my labor with everyone.

Test your colors here on the samples from
"My Pocket Coloring Companion"
&
"My Coloring Companion"

www.ingramcontent.com/pod-product-compliance
Lightning Source LLC
Chambersburg PA
CBHW082341220526
45470CB00008B/2591